THAT Girl

Where Did She Go and How Do I Find Her?

Stephanie Connors

THAT Girl; Where Did She Go and How Do I Find Her?
Copyright © 2020 by (Stephanie Connors)

All rights reserved. No part of this book may be reproduced or transmitted in any form or by any means without written permission from the author.

ISBN 9798363123542

The information provided in this book, THAT Girl, should not be used for diagnosing or treating a health problem or disease, and those seeking personal medical advice should consult with a licensed physician. Always seek the advice of your doctor or other qualified health provider regarding any medical condition.

Midnight
by Stephanie Connors
July 2020

I don't think I will ever have THAT kind of strength again. As I review every month in my mind – my eyes water, my heart stings, I can't breathe.

With each passing month, I ebb between gladness and sorrow. I push through. My mind fogs some, and I'm grateful. Clarity hurts. To believe in Truth and then have it snatched away is a punch, confusing at best.

I know that stillness heals. Not at first, but in time. Though kindness is at bay, I reach and hope for connection.

When darkness falls, I refuse to give in. I stay alert. I stay here.

I am tender under the weight. I see you too. There is more. The work, the very hard work, and the claiming pay off. Let's finish well. Forgive.

Jump start tomorrow. Keep believing this path is good and necessary and yours. Announce it. The line no longer matters.

I hear the cheers. 5, 4, 3, 2, 1

Preface

It was quite the year, wasn't it? 2020. The high hopes of the year were seemingly put out of sight almost as soon as the ball dropped. It was March for most. For me, sooner.

The time was shortly after 2am Sunday morning January 5, 2020. I don't remember a dream, a vision, or even a nightmare specifically. What I do remember is dread. A sadness, a knowing, a warning.

I woke suddenly, gasping for air, crying. It was my own sobbing that woke me. There was an ache so deep in my gut. I tucked in, tried fetal, but could not ease my pain. My husband jolted upright with concern. "Something's wrong." I shared. "Something is really wrong."

I collapsed back to sleep as quickly as I had awakened. But in the morning, I silently recalled my experience. That hard to fathom, hard to interpret, harder to retell experience.

I don't know if I would, or could, have done anything differently in the months immediately following that wee hour moment. But had I realized that alarming was for me, perhaps for all of us, maybe I could have been braced.

Now, after seeing the year through and all it entailed, I believe it happened as it should. (*My journey, at least.*) The good, the bad, the retching and the beautiful. Stay with me.

THAT Girl

Where Did She Go and How Do I Find Her?

Stephanie Connors

Introduction

THAT girl.

It would be far too easy to say she was gone, or she went missing. I know that would not be true. I know she's there. Still. She's waiting.

Let's go get her!

1

There's a time in all of our lives when we face crisis. Some more often than not. Me – I was in that 'too often' group. I craved peace. But having only seen glimpses, I got lost.

Lost in the searching, lost in the suffering, just lost.

You see, I didn't even recognize peace when it was within reach. My preference, my 'go to', was to run away; physically, emotionally, mostly both. I was more comfortable living my 'picture' of life, rather than facing and living the messy life I created.

But all that changed this past year. This unimaginable, unprecedented, mixed-up year. Ya, you know the one.

The work to get 'her' was real and hard, very hard. There is no denying that to ignore 'her' would have been simpler, certainly a less contentious path. But that, my friend, was not for me. There was a new course calling me. I was scared. I was grieving. I was choiceless.

I stand here today a different person than I was that *midnight*, New Year's 2020. I have taken back myself, my *truest* self; or at least as much as I am able to date.

Still, I am pulled to keep searching, to stay in pursuit. Perhaps that is our job, perhaps discovering and appreciating our birth is exactly our destiny.

I purpose, *we connect with our creator and discover how unique, how one-of-a-kind, we are inside and out. Then love, and be loved, as fashioned.*

Healing and wholeness can happen. You are not in this life alone. Although, alone is ok, and even quite necessary for a season.

I will share what I learned to find 'her'. And I invite you to journey with me today.

2

Just because you don't remember that time, doesn't mean you didn't live it. That twirling about in your gingham dress, that rocking your baby doll close to your chest, that 'make-believe' time. We were there, living and breathing those precious moments. Those moments when we were free, unhindered, raw.

Of course, childhood is never perfect. Far from perfect for most. Worn and tattered, we press on until we emerge as these unrecognizable adults put together with all the effort we can muster. Effort that comes and goes throughout the years, making life manageable, while making life numb.

But I suggest we are not shattered, not broken beyond repair. We are neither our diagnosis, or lack thereof. We are just dormant, covered in memories and experiences that became larger than who we were at seed.

The rooting and digging up is intense. It is primal and nauseating and madness at times. It is also soothing and comforting and real.

Beneath the layers of hurt, the layers of denial and shame exists our true self. The person who our creator designed. The person we are meant to be, and without us the universe cries. We must do everything to allow this human to emerge. For our core being, our very purpose, our inborn and innermost power is love. And that power, love, can heal us, our neighbor, the world.

3

I have missed the mark over and over again; in romance, in family relationships, in community and career. But where I failed most, *until now*, was in knowing myself, my own needs, my dreams, my individual preferences, my fears. And without that knowledge, I blindly lived life. I was unable to determine what would fulfill me because I did not know who I was or what made me whole.

Spiritually, I knew my home. But apart from that certainty, I was unacquainted with the depths of my maker's masterpiece: me.

You see, when we are a stranger to ourselves, unaware of our needs, our vulnerabilities, it is impossible to be truly close with another. *Who* are we sharing with them? How do we build intimacy when we are unknown even to ourselves? How do we express needs we do not know exist?

Only after studying and learning ourselves will we discover our brilliance, our weaknesses and our gifting to the world. At that point, once versed, we can begin to reveal our thoughts and verbalize our desires. We become satisfied, and our relationships bloom because they are true, authentic and real.

4

What has done the most damage to my life, and my loves, is making incompatible choices that did not line up with my intention. Somewhere along the way from cradle to adulthood, my self-worth fell flat on its face. And from that place of fear, I went about carving my identity and staking my ground. The conclusions I drew from my self-talk led me to doubt who I was and what I was capable of doing; and not doing.

This dialogue coupled with divorced parents and a runaway mom did not bode well for a healthy start. Add in hormones and acne, there lied a recipe for a mess. My mess. The one I finally own now.

Having grown-up in the 70's and 80s, my view of society was limited to my local neighborhood, the Brady's and my own imagination.

I played the "Mystery Date" game as if my life depended on it, and I always chose the 'family' road in the "Game of Life"; hoping beyond hope to pack in as many peg children my car would allow. I played 'school', I played 'house' and I dabbled with dance.

But my happy place, my deepest contentment was found in the pew of my family church. In the quiet, in the discipline, among the incense and song, I was 'home'.

Some say I 'found religion' at a time of great pain in my life, but the truth is that for as long as I remember I have always had communion with my God. I am grateful. I am honored.

All of this - my era, my town, my heritage, my belonging or not - formed my personality, my sense of self, my lens.

I leaped into my twenties a cross between Julie Andrews and Madonna, unsure of where I fit on that spectrum. I muddled through the next decades; mistakes numerous along the way.

Today as I write, I know most of the muddling was meaningful, some unnecessary, but all a rite of passage of sorts. For few, growing pains are minor, even undetectable for less, but for me and for most, they were tough and true. Yet, this latest season served as a time to learn about myself, to heal and grow, and now I hope to pass my lessons on to you.

5

I won't drag you down my every bad turn or dark alley. You have your own past, your own story, which is unique and powerful. I will share a glimpse, enough to know you can relate, but not enough to overwhelm or bury. Through my brevity, if you find we have walked a similar path, linger if you choose, for a while. But be open to write a fresh refrain, a new song. Our common ground will connect us and initiate trust so you can process, move through and ultimately cast new vision.

SO... to bring you up to speed, current day, I'll hit the highlights and leave the rest private. You see, this history, this roller coaster of my life not only took me for a ride, there were passengers too. Hate is a strong word and I hate to use it. But I hate that my actions hurt the people I love most. I would say that the shame of that truth was the hardest part of my emotional recovery. A new concept for me I learned was self-compassion. I'm still working on this practice today. I know that forgiveness usually requires repetition, almost always. When that twinge in our heart resurfaces, we must forgive, again. And again. Perhaps forever, we forgive. Not just others, by ourselves.

My list of hurts I caused may shock you or bring comfort to you knowing that you are not alone in your pit. You may be out now too, but if not, remember, there is a way. My way will be different than yours and that is ok. Use what works, leave the rest.

Here goes: There were a series of decisions during those chill years of the late 80's and early 90's that led me down a road of questionable situations, difficult circumstances, and at times self-sabotage. Free will is never freer than in our twenties, or at least that was my tale.

After graduating college one semester late, I headed to sunny Florida to start a new life, and a new destiny. Up until that point, life had dealt me a few bad hands, but I dug deep and kept a bright future in sight. I had a wonderful high school experience and still cherish many friendships to this very day. These girls are all warriors in their own right. They have won their own battles, and they are stronger for the fight. They are genuine, hilarious, and they will have your back without question. But, the most treasured quality, to me, of these friendships is nonjudgment; something so rare these days it only makes me love and respect these women that much more. They were part of my healing which I will share more on later.

Back to my story…. I arrived in Clearwater, Florida, excited, confident, but mostly naïve. It was winter 1988. With the surf in front of me and the long, cold winters of the northeast behind me, I was ready. Ready to start over, ready to begin again, simply ready. I loved the warmth of the sun on my face, I still do. If I feel the sun even near me, I close my eyes and lean in to its embrace. It's not just the pink tint to my cheeks that I love, it is how it energizes me.

I knew if none of my other dreams came true in my life, I would have this one. I picked where I wanted to live. I live in Florida. Check.

I started out on the west coast of Florida, the Tampa Bay area, where I met the love of my life, my dear and treasured husband, Kevin. Later, I moved to the northeast coast of Florida, then the southeast and now back again to the northeast where I pray, I stay.

Life is good now. I am settled and content. I am happy. I know people tout that joy is the emotion to strive for so that even when life's toughest battles rear their head, we can keep an inner peace. That is true and I am thankful to possess joy, yet I am not ashamed to say I am happy also. Getting here was not easy and my scars are many. I welcome both emotions.

I have more than I need in a material way. That has never been on my radar anyway. I am thrilled to have the bills paid on time, not early, but on time, and I have three squares a day, sometimes more. I don't have a retirement plan, and I am not getting any younger, but I am still content. I love what I do. Teach, write, care for others.

I am happy because -well, simply, why not? Really!! I mean I have been putting happy off it seems my whole life. Waiting to reach that number on a scale, scheming how to build that custom log cabin in the country, daydreaming about destinations that make your hair curl. Enough already. Enough.

Without too much detail, let's just say by the time I HAD to heal, I was an expert at hiding. Hiding my pain, hiding my past, and hiding even from myself. I was so used to putting on the brave face that I fully convinced myself all was well, when in fact, it wasn't.

Two abusive husbands = two divorces, narrowing escapes, a stint in a domestic violence shelter residence, court dates, two births, one miscarriage, the death of my last parent, food banks, broken down cars, second jobs, third jobs, it all took its toll. Yet, if it weren't for this mess, I would not know this happiness now.

I marvel at the resilience of the human body. This shutting down period, this 'ignoring period' saved my life. If I had to be present with all this mess at the time, I would have crumbled. I am thankful and in awe of how our bodily systems can compartmentalize for a season so we can be productive and do what we need to do to function, to parent, to work, to cook, to drive, to simply even bathe sometimes. *Have you been there?* It was sheer survival for me then to set aside this pain so I could care for my children and household. I remember anytime I 'got present', frankly it was too much and I would collapse under the weight. There was no time or space for that experience. There was no room for disruption. Time for sorting and grieving and healing had to come later.

I couldn't effectively deal with these emotions until recent, until my life was steeped with true love and I had a safe environment to process and become. Think how remarkable our brains are to do that, to determine when to protect and delay, when to forge and heal. My body cared for me almost on autopilot so I could do what needed done at the time.

I used to just hate how I handled those times, but after studying trauma, I realized that the process is miraculous really. It kept my mind safe until I could get in a better place to work through the trauma. I have done that now and I will share with you how I did my recovery. I am not a professional, I am just a woman who at the point of crisis HAD to finally process all that I had done and all that was done to me.

One of my greatest lessons has been *self-compassion*. I care about and for others who are hurting and I easily empathize with their plight. But myself, that was different. Although I had read about self-compassion, I never practiced it. And then one day, it dawned on me to look at myself sort of from outside my own body. If I knew 'that girl', if 'that girl' was my friend, what would I do for her? That's when the blinders fell off. You see, I would love her, take gentle care of her, be kind to her, feed her well, beautify her, and most importantly speak kindly to her and forgive her. This was a turning point for me. You will get there too.

The following are my steps, my journey, to the present me, to 'that girl', to the woman who was meant to be from the beginning. I have dealt with and integrated my wounds. I am whole. I am forgiven. I am free.

6

The first thing I did was recognize I could not do this by myself. I needed help. The hurt was too much, the pain too deep. I could not just brush myself off and plunge through life. Not anymore. I was in despair.

I sought and found an in-person counselor. I wanted to get a 'live' professional perspective of what I had been through and how to get to the other side. Again, without insurance, or spare financial resources, I had to think outside the box.

I recalled a time when a domestic violence shelter came to my rescue. So, I went to the website of the domestic violence organization in my community. I was thrilled to see they offered counseling; both one on one and group counseling. I called to set up an appointment.

It was an intake session with a kind, gentle woman. As he asked questions, and I answered them, I was overwhelmed with just gratitude for this opportunity to tell my story. I was heard. Not a single word was spoken that didn't accompany a tear. She listened carefully and assigned me a match. I had an appointment a few days later in their 'secret' location.

The hurt, that wake-up call I experienced earlier in the year had surfaced here. I was raw, inconsolable at times. She listened. She took notes. She had heard these stories probably thousands of times, but she made me feel like my story was her first and that my truth mattered.

The counseling was free. FREE. Again, I share this because do not let money or lack of it determine your emotional or mental health. You do have to get out there and find it. That takes strength and vulnerability, but you must muster up this courage and get talking.

I only met her once in person. I still believe it was a pre-ordained meeting, a divine appointment. Remember, this is early 2020. Late February to be precise. Covid-19 shortly took hold nationwide and the shelter closed its in-person counseling operations. Welcome Zoom.

Who knew what this pandemic would present? I now had a counselor via Zoom to see me through, even to this present day. Imagine that! I had the opportunity to meet her in 'real life' before 'real life' became rare and video became the 'new norm'. The timing astounds me still. Now, we would meet one on one via screen. It worked. I was grateful.

She was a stranger, but not for long. Week by week, I poured out my pain, my heartache, my life. It wasn't pretty, but the tears flowed and I soon realized this release was way overdue. She validated my feelings. I needed that probably the most. She confirmed that how I was feeling was normal and natural, and she understood. Her point of view was from a world of experience counseling women just like me. I no longer felt broken beyond repair. It would take work, and time, but healing was available.

The program she chose for my healing was called Seeking Safety. There were handouts to read and discuss and worksheets to complete. Now, we were getting somewhere. The homework was so helpful to me, and ultimately to my family. Having to be accountable to someone gave me structure for my healing. The homework, the study and reflection, were different than anything I've ever took on. It was actually self-care. And self-care was new for me. I mean I got pedicures regularly and got my grays covered as I could afford, but this self-care was different. This self-care was about my emotions and my inner life. It was weird. It was scary. It was essential.

In addition to the structured Seeking Safety program, I had a few other tools too. The first tool was a self-care calendar where I planned time for myself. It wasn't just the activities themselves that were healing, it was making myself a priority in my day. The revelation was that my personal self-care was just as important, or more, than laundry, grocery shopping or cooking. When I started looking at myself as someone to love and care for, my outlook changed. I loved so many people, now I had to take that same energy and love *me*. These 'activities" ranged from a morning quiet time to read with a hot beverage, or a set aside time to exercise, or wearing a face mask for 15 minutes, or my favorite - an Epsom Salt soak in the tub. I was on the schedule every day. I wasn't last. I was a priority.

Second, I had a success journal where I logged the emotional successes that I accomplished each week such as creating and sticking to a healthy boundary, addressing a need I had and getting it met, enjoying my hobbies like reading and writing, or physical accomplishments such as exercising, eating well, sleeping well and other healthy choices.

Journaling is key to maintaining good emotional health too. When overwhelmed or stressed, write, write, write. You do not need to be grammatically correct, or spell right, just get your thoughts out of your head. I heard a morning 'dump' is best. I try to keep this process today.

The Seeking Safety Model itself was a good fit for me. I had lived for so many years feeling unsafe. I couldn't quite name that feeling before taking this course so I was relieved to know what was manifesting inside me. I knew I had to take back my power and see a safe world so I could heal and live. I had to figure out what safe meant for me and go about creating that environment – no matter what.

7

The most important step, I think, came next. Like any devoted individual in recovery, I had to admit my problem. I had experienced trauma. Me? What? Trauma? Yes, that was the name of what I went through. My state/ condition.

Once I figured that I had experienced trauma (suggested by a loved one I must add), I went out to research all I could find on the subject. The internet is FULL of resources. I quickly found a 7-day summit on trauma recovery and enrolled. It was FREE just for those seven days. I devoured it.

In fact, we were on our summer vacation in Maine when I discovered this summit. I toyed with not doing it as I thought 'working' on a holiday would be counterproductive, but it was quite the opposite. I had time and space to give this time the intensity it required, and deserved. Notebook in hand, I watched each daily session and took massive notes. I couldn't believe how they 'knew' me, how my mind worked now (post trauma) and how my body reacted to life and its situations. I hung on the speakers' every word. The lessons were coming at me like a fire hose and I couldn't seem to take it all in.

I learned about the fight, flight, freeze and fawn responses and how I was undoubtedly stuck in these modes. Each felt familiar to me albeit they surfaced at different times, or in different scenarios. I learned the whys and ways of my condition. I learned about fragmentation and how our mind and body suppress experiences for our own good, for our survival. I was thankful for that innate ability. I learned I could not live in the present while tending to these suppressed traumas at the same time. I discovered how to integrate these experiences and heal. I am not qualified to go into any of these topics in any depth, but I urge you to explore these concepts I mention.

At the end of the seven-day workshop, the host offered the Trauma Summit for sale. You could own and reference this material forever. I needed this so much. The cost was affordable, yet we did not have extra at that time. It was mid-summer 2020; our finances, like so many, reflected the Covid-19 times and its consequential economic impact. I noticed the scholarship tab in the menu and applied. After submitting an application along with an essay, I am beyond grateful that I was awarded a full scholarship for the summit. It also came with bonus material, extra interviews, handouts and more. This was a turning point for me. I understood that what I went through and what happened to my brain and nervous system was real and painful and raw. I was validated. My feelings mattered. I would heal.

I since became a member of this organization and will buy resources not only to help myself, but to support their cause and show my appreciation for my scholarship.

The organization is Sounds True and their website is: www.soundstrue.com. If you are in a position to donate, please consider. From their website *"At Sounds True we believe that everyone has the right to access transformational tools and teachings to build greater resilience, compassion, and freedom."* Wow! I have so much respect for this organization and its intention. Again, thanks for considering a donation.

I understand that ideally an in-person therapist who specializes in trauma would be best, but when budgets are tight, or like us, live uninsured, there are reasonable options available. Mental health is not just a buzz word or trend, it is the bedrock of existence. Many physical ailments stem RIGHT from a mental or emotional illness.

Get help. The stigma has faded. Gather your circle. Take a chance and be vulnerable with others. Build your support team. Choose well.

Your 'team' might look different than you expected, but that's ok. Surround yourself with genuine, authentic folks who encourage you to be real, open and true. If you find judgement or negativity, they are not your people, at least for now. If you can't find your few, let's go get some. (More on that in a later chapter).

There are a lot of resources out there. Don't stay stuck. Find a method or model, a program or person, that works for you. A community for you exists and awaits.

8

After a good hard look inside, I realized I needed more balance in my approach to recovery and healing. The reason I use the word recovery so much is simply, I like it. It fits.

According to Google's English Dictionary recovery is defined as: "1. A return to a normal state of health, mind, strength. 2. The action or process of regaining possession or control of something stolen or lost." That's right. We are working on returning to 'that girl' who was stolen or lost, or maybe never even had a chance to be born. Step by step, we'll get there, together.

After the trauma summit and all it revealed, I decided to take a plunge into another area of recovery. In part, this next step in healing is the most exciting and rewarding stage because the work is tangible and more easily notice by others.

The process began when I met a doctor at a networking meeting who practiced alternative medicine. I made an appointment.

You see, I was so busy working on my emotional health, that I didn't address the toll the trauma took on my body and physical health. I know traditional medical doctors and conventional medicine may be more comfortable for some of you, and I too am a fan of annual check-ups, blood work, baseline numbers and scans. For me personally, I just didn't want to go to a traditional medical doctor and have them prescribe me something without first exploring all other options. I didn't want to mask symptoms or numb straggling worries. I wanted to discover, confront and remove the root cause.

She had an affordable monthly short-term program where she would see me twice a month to check my well-being. Every so many visits, my vitals such as BMI, heart rate, weight, etc. would be evaluated. The program also included individualized nutritional counseling, food sensitivity testing and custom supplementation.

I started the program in June 2021 and I am showing improvement in all areas, particularly in the symptom check area. I am sleeping better, I have less anxiety, my moods are more stable. My skin, nails and hair look great. I still have work to do in order to decrease my BMI and lower my resting heartbeat, but I've made progress and I'm motivated for more. I'm convince that the steady weight loss will prove easier to KEEP off.

Overall, I love just the fact I am fueling my body properly. I keep a food log where I track my food, water, supplements, and exercise. I have not lost all the weight yet that I want to lose, but I am making smart food choices. It feels so good knowing my food is helping me and not harming me. I have been eating this way long enough now that I rarely crave junk or sweets. I just make one good food choice after another (the majority of the time) and trust that my body is healing itself.

It's worth reiterating here. I am not a health professional by any means. I'm just sharing my experience and some tidbits I gathered along the way. Please consult and follow your own doctor's advice on all health, dietary and medical matters.

So, back to basics. I am big on hydrating; at least 8 glasses of water a day. I do have a hot coffee with almond milk in the morning. A magical must! If coffee is not your thing, or you would like to try a different wake-up beverage that boasts health benefits, consider Matcha. It is a favorite of mine too.

I learned from the nutritionist that the best 'meal' or 'snack' is one that includes: a healthy carbohydrate, a protein, and a healthy fat. (CPF.... That is my 'mantra'!) **C**: I learned that healthy carbohydrates include: fruit, vegetables, brown rice and sweet potatoes. There are even some healthy carbs that double as protein sources such as: quinoa, legumes/ beans/ lentils and non-fat plain Greek yogurt.

P: My protein comes through collagen protein powder, lean meats, nuts, nut butter, shellfish and eggs. I love eggs hard boiled on salad! I am trying to incorporate other fish too like salmon and cod.

F: I also learned that all fat is not bad. I learned there are good fats which include avocados, avocado oil, olives, olive oil. I make my salad dressing homemade now using organic olive oil, organic balsamic vinegar, a little water and the Good Season Italian Seasoning Packet. YUM!

Smoothies are my ultimate CPF go-to. It's that nutrient combination that makes my shake recipe ideal. I make a fairly large one in the blender around 5pm at night. I drink half before dinner and then I put the second half in a mason jar and seal the lid tight. I place it on the top shelf of the refrigerator, against the wall where it freezes ever so slightly. I will drink that frosty smoothie for breakfast the next morning.

My recipe: '

- 2 scoops of collagen protein powder

-fruit (blueberries or strawberries – organic frozen)

-half an avocado (frozen also - makes it so creamy!)

-organic spinach

-1 tablespoon of Organic milled flaxseed

-almond milk

Viola: CPF shake!

Nutrition Tip: Limit or AVOID white bread, pastas, sugar, also anything processed (in a box or bag). You get the picture. Choose food that nourishes the body and directs it to its highest level of function. Remember the recovery definition above: "a return to a normal state of health, mind, strength."

You might wonder.... *Do I ever deviate from this eating style?* Sure!! And that's ok. It's only every once in a while, and I usually plan on it. I actually schedule what I am craving as a "treat' meal or dessert. Confession: I used to do 'treat weekends, *every* weekend, so just a meal/ dessert is a big change.

I can tell you that all this adjustment is so worth the effort. I enjoy being more in control of my intake versus it controlling me. As the late health and fitness guru Jack LaLanne would say "Live to eat, don't eat to live."

I believe the rewards of healthy eating are as beneficial mentally as physically. By accomplishing your goals, you raise your self-confidence and self-esteem which will lead to a healthier version of you. And that new you will make better choices all around for your future.

What does this "food talk" have to do with trauma? LOTS! When your body is functioning at its personal best, your brain has its optimal chance to heal from trauma. Recovery takes all you got and you need the tools to follow through with the work. A healthy body is your greatest tool and foundation.

Recovery is deepest when the mind, body, and spirit all heal; separately and also together. These areas crave concentrated care, but ultimately peace dwells when all three operate in harmony.

Personally, I suggest focused care separately at first, then together. My order was spirit, mind, body. Your path is unique and could be different. Be assured that each of these parts (spirit, mind, body) will cooperate with your efforts. These parts were designed to work in unison. You were created to be whole. I think that is the meaning of wholeness. No separation between these three parts of yourself. No brokenness. You'll know when they are in sync. *How?* You'll just know.

9

BMI. Body Mass Index. Well, this marker seems to be where I am currently stuck. As I stated before, I am not a healthcare professional, just a woman in my late fifties trying to live long and strong. What I have read about BMI is that the number determines what percentage of your weight is from muscle and what percentage of your weight is from fat. A high BMI could indicate visceral fat that would harm your organs and cause diseases. Visceral fat meaning fat inside your body that surrounds your organs that doesn't necessarily show on the outside. Thin folks can also have visceral fat.

My number is not alarming, but it needs to improve. Disclosure here. I have not been an exercise fan for some years now; mostly due to my scoliosis. I danced in my childhood, teen, and young adult years for which I am very grateful. I really think this foundation kept my scoliosis in check until middle age. I also made lifelong friendships from all these outlets. And speaking of friendships, there is one in particular that offered life changing counsel.

While away on a girls' trip, a reunion of high school friends, I received a nugget of wisdom. This counsel came from a dear friend who is a Pilates instructor. She graciously offered her time at our 'retreat' to give an exercise class on the beach. She encouraged us to go after a more active lifestyle on a regular basis and gave examples of how we could work exercise into our daily lives. I shared with her my limitations and also my hesitancy to join her class. It is then she shared about Pilates and how this form of exercise could be a solution for me. She was so understanding and compassionate. It was evident she had passion for her calling and had seen results in similar people. She gave me tips for my posture which I implemented immediately, and I try to be mindful of them daily.

After the girls' weekend and upon return to my home town, I decide to seek out a Pilates studio. After two sample classes, I join. It isn't the least expensive exercise compared to some gyms out there, but by far, it packs the needed punch.

It has done so much for me. It has improved my strength, flexibility, and stamina. My sciatica is gone!! If you have ever struggled with sciatica, you know how precious this healing is to experience. I do Reformer classes, both Flow 1 and Center and Balance. If you are unfamiliar, it focuses around using a 'bed' type machine, a pulley system and many other pieces of equipment.

The very best and unexpected joy of Pilates to me has been self-confidence. I can DO it! I can exercise!! I have crossed over from a non-exercising person to all in. I am grateful and encourage you to give it a try if you can.

So, as I keep moving toward my goal weight, I will keep up with Pilates. I am staying consistent and hopeful that my BMI will improve as my muscle mass increases, all in due time. I know there is no quick fix to change this number. I am in it for the long haul. Steady practice, committed days, month after month, progress will happen.

There are other ways to improve your BMI number, but I am no expert here. My hope was just to bring your attention to this matter. It is more about the ratio than the number on the scale. My advice would be to try different things until you find what you love. You are more apt to stay disciplined if you love your exercise of choice. Mix it up even. Perhaps commit to a time and place, but not a particular activity. Say "I will exercise at 5pm everyday in my living room." Or "I will exercise at 9am everyday in my yard." Just saying it will help to form a neural pathway to achieving those goals.

You do NOT have to pay money to exercise. There are many free types of movement you can do, so keep searching. Walking, climbing stairs, or a simple dance party in your kitchen – free and fun! All of these movements make you a more active person and this activity will not only help your waistline; it will improve your mental and emotional health. Write me. Share your ideas. I am rooting for you!

10

Well, it was my turn. 1/16/2022. Since the beginning, through the birth of this book and to that very day, I had yet to fall prey to its clutches. That's right. Covid-19. *How could I not write about this unprecedented season of our lifetime?*

My lesson, my takeaway is 'never think it can't happen to you.' We are not invincible as a nation, as a family or as individuals. Fortunately, I had a mild case.

I am beyond blessed to have a mature, independent daughter and a self-less, loving husband who could care for themselves as I healed. They made my meals and 'delivered' them to the bedroom I was quarantined in. They brought me flowers to brighten my nightstand and they spoke loving thoughts when they cracked open the door to check on me. I felt loved, and safe. I realize this is not the experience all had and my heart grieves those sorrows.

I remember the 'news' clearly. It was February 2020. I was working virtually for a company based in Beijing, China. I was teaching the most precious children from ages 4 years to 16 years or so. I was an 'English as a Second Language' teacher, ESL for short.

The virus swooped in fast, in their country. They were all on lockdown. I didn't even know what that meant, at first. My employer asked us to film an encouraging video for our students and post it to our profile. I remember feeling such compassion for them being in their apartments fearing this contagious and deadly new virus outside. The schools were shut down, and they had to move to an online classroom in addition to my tutoring. Parents were working from home too. One student's mother was working in another part of the country and could not come home. They were scared. I was scared for them. I loved them. Most had been my students for a few years now. I watched them grow.

As I prepared this video, I fought back tears as I rehearsed. I remember clearly how I encouraged them to stay strong. I told them how I was thinking of them and their country often. Those pronouns 'them' and 'their'. I recall thinking it's 'their' situation. It never, ever dawned on me that it would touch us. Not our invincible country and definitely not our family, or myself. I shake my head as I write this thinking of how arrogant I was that day to think I was somehow so special that it would not affect me. Well, it now has done so. Mildly, I am grateful.

Just an odd time to live...don't you think? I will never again take for granted that what happens across the globe could not happen here. The losses have been so great around the world. I have learned a lot and made adjustments twice over. I was vigilant with my health to build my immune system. I rebuilt my circles because life is short and I want others around me to be those I truly love and feel loved by. I reframed my faith in ways that would take a second book. I finally,

FINALLY now sweat the small stuff less. And I am so grateful to be one of the ones still here after all those who were taken. If you are reading this book, you are here too. Make the most of this life. You got another chance.

11

I have a lot to share about this next topic and piece of healing. Community. There is nothing better than being surrounded by people you love and who reciprocate those feelings. We all need relationships brimming with mutual love, respect and acceptance. We need connections that improve our well-being, and encourage our growth. We need caring conversations that build each other up, bring healing to our hearts and a salve to our soul.

I have learned it is better to be alone than to be with the wrong people. What I mean by 'wrong' people is human beings who put you personally into 'fight, flight, freeze, or fawn' mode. Let me clarify. Just because someone is 'wrong' for you, doesn't mean they're a 'bad' person or that they're ''wrong' for everyone. It just means your two nervous systems don't bring out the best in each other. You need to find folks you can co-regulate with together. Co-regulate in layman's terms would mean the experience people have when they are with another that makes BOTH of them feel safe, calm and at peace.

I am no psychologist, but I do know that before I did this trauma work, I was in a permanent fight or flight stage, sometimes freeze phase, and had an occasional appearance of fawn. Being stuck in these modes is so unhealthy, not only emotionally, but physically. I had to work hard to change this situation. My life depended on it. My blood pressure was too high. My father died from a fatal heart attack at age 50. I'm 56 at the moment. I want to stay here for my husband and children as long as destined. I had to do my part.

I did not want to medicate away this problem, unless other means failed, so this 'lowering' had to take precedence. Rethinking my circle was not just for my mental health, it was for survival.

I began to evaluate my tribe, or tribes really. I realized I used to have segments of friends more than just a single core group of women. I remember this being the norm of my childhood and adolescence; neighborhood friends, dance friends, school friends, work friends, church friends.

My style narrowed over the years. If I were going to return to 'that girl' I had to go back in time and recreate what made be happy – pre-trauma. I had a diverse group of lovely friends in different pockets of my life. I realized within those different circles, there were many personalities and that made life fun. I loved that!

There will be those with whom you will have an instant, almost divine connection. Cherish them. Some you may not be super close with even after considerable time together, but that's ok. I don't think you need to be super close to every one of these folks in your circles, but you can be friendly and see where the relationship grows. And there may be a few that you recognize that keeping them at arm's length is the right choice for you.

Relationships, in general, got really dicey and divided for a while in 2020. This could still be the case for you. If so, let's get busy. Let's get clear on who you want in your life.

I withdrew. That's not my norm, but I now see how that withdrawal served a purpose. I guess it started with the March '2-week Florida lockdown'. My family at first had a blast with this time. It was new and refreshing to be home together night after night, not running here and there to different activities.

Every night, my sweet daughter created a 'restaurant' on our screen porch. She worked all day making homemade decorations and menus and the food matched the décor. It was a precious time, really. At first.

She wore an apron and played waitress. Each evening (for a week), my husband and I had romantic dates on our lanai. We tipped well too. We had cuisines and experiences from around the world, complete with matching music.

We also created an outdoor barbershop where she cut my husband's hair. She did great! I reciprocated and thanked her by treating her to a spa day and an afternoon tea, at home, of course.

We never imagined this time period or trial would last. But it did. In fact, on 1/20/22, it touched our house; almost *two years* from that very first home 'restaurant'.

One thing after another seemed to pile up on us individually and collectively, yet we kept moving along, trudging forward. With in-person social situations limited, I dove deeper into social media to stay connected. Facebook primarily…. par for my age group. I am grateful, really. It was mostly positive interactions, but it was also there where I saw women I have loved, trusted and even admired share views that frankly shocked me, mostly saddened me.

I know some may hide behind keyboards to be bolder or make a statement, but this was not the case. A handful of times, I reached out to the women who shared such posts and I was crushed by their response to me. I might have just asked them what they really meant and their replies were basically that what I read matched their hearts. Now, you may be thinking I was just personally offended, or had a difference of opinion. This was different.

My world, specifically one particular circle that I had known for over a decade, was unraveling. Today, I'm glad. I am glad the masks came off people in this season and I got to see true colors. And even more glad I made a change.

This may seem harsh, but if after all this healing, I could not be authentic to myself, then what have I really learned? I could no longer be entrenched in these circles knowing what I know now. To stay quiet, I would be a hypocrite. To speak out, would just cause division, pain, and a setback for me personally.

I observed and I recognized my need to rebuild. I set about my task. First, I pulled back and waited. The friends in my life who I knew shared common values stayed, and the ones who made it clear our virtues differ are no longer a regular part of my life. This season was tough, but it pointed the way for this 'circle change' and for that one detail, I am grateful.

So, for me, I lost people from Covid in a different way. And that's ok. The friends who remained are my 'ride or dies' and I love them. They are the ones who believe in me, support my life choices and whose lives align with my values. They bring out the best in me in a variety of ways. They cheer me on. It's mutual. There are a few views we hold differently, but we have talked them through and are comfortable enough to give each other the respect to see life differently. But we are real with one another, genuine to our truths and we hold no judgement. That is key to me. No judgement. Just be there, authentically, nothing fake, no pretense. I am blessed.

Now, here's where things get sticky. I had to stretch myself this time. Think outside the box. Consider every person a potential friend as she came into my life. It was even a bit fun when I look back. A spirit of inclusion, love and non-judgement was my prerequisites, per say. It was my 'line in the sand' of sorts. To me, that had to be the foundation of any new friendship.

You see, I know, really know, that I am imperfect, a hot mess at times, for certain. I believe it is not our human place to judge others, good or bad. It's a rather new practice for me, but my greatest goal. My background promoted judging and it was habit. I couldn't see clearly.... until I did. Then, I had to rid myself of that ugliness. I am a work in progress.

I can't hold others to any standard, and I am thankful for that reciprocity. When we invest without strings, or agendas, that's love to me. When we are fully ourselves, when we are real and raw, and expose that vulnerability to each other without judgment, that's connection to me. Pretense and pretending have no place in these relationships. You will know when you find them. They will feel like home.

12

Circle changing. That's my made-up buzz word. Once you acknowledge your need for new circles, it's time. Maybe you can stay connected on a surface level with those who no longer serve your health, but that's is a personal choice. You don't need to have a formal 'break up' or share an announcement. Just move forward with finding new affirming folks.

Where to start? I'll share my process. It's a bit bumpy, but worth the twists and turns. I did not abruptly leave some and cleave to others. The change was gradual, it's ongoing, and will continue to evolve. I simply explored different groups in my town and slowly made changes as I found a natural fit.

Prior to this transition in my life, I had 'all my eggs in one basket', well the majority anyway. That mindset had to change because when my basket broke, so did my heart.

I joined two new groups, intentionally both secular. Each group a game changer in different ways. The first one was eye opening, convicting, life altering. It was an online group called Community Conversations. It was a 2 hour Zoom meeting every Tuesday. I wept like a baby at the close of my first session. I have come out of my bubble, and social darkness now.

Do you want to find new community and make genuine, lasting connections? Be intentional. Start somewhere. For this group in particular, I reached out to a neighbor and acquaintance who I remembered held these core values I was looking to find in others. I sent her a bold, almost desperate message. She replied with such compassion and understanding that I knew I made the right decision to reach out to her for direction. She contacted the leader of this group and shortly I received an email invitation.

The group consists of 40 some members from different backgrounds, cultures, and perspectives. It is a melting pot of my county, not my tiny beach town or suburb, but my county as a whole. In essence, it's a picture of our country and represents our world.

I love the format of this meeting. We start by taking turns reading the communication guidelines and how they apply to our interactions. The conversations flow with these guidelines in mind. In general, the guidelines layout how to respectfully have a discussion on perhaps a sensitive topic.

The guidelines in simple terms inform participants how to dialogue. Examples: Listen to the person speaking and even 'try on' their point of view. Use 'I' statements such as "I believe" or "I feel" rather than speaking as *the* authority on a matter. You can actually find the specifics on their website.

Not only are these guidelines good for the group, I believe they are good for everyday life and relationships. I try to use these principals often, but I could do better. I'm growing and maturing, which is the important part. So are you!

Now, the leader of the group emails the participants a few days prior to the meeting. The email outlines the topic of the meeting and often includes an article to read or a video to view in advance pertaining to the topic. We always conclude each meeting with an opportunity for participants to call out and thank others who contributed something to the group that touched them personally.

Sometimes, we even do breakout sessions where the participants are divided into smaller groups say less than ten. That's when the walls come down and we share our deep feelings without fear of judgement, condemnation or criticism. I have heard stories and testimonies I would never have heard elsewhere. I can only describe this experience as beautiful, poignant, and rare.

I have learned SO much being a part of this group. I offer a copy the guidelines with others when they share that they are having difficulty discussing things with people of opposing views. I hope my small contribution helps my nook of the world, even just an inch.

If you are interested in participating in or hosting a Community Conversations group, information is available on the internet. There you can find a local group to join or find out how to start one in your area. Go once. Promise yourself that. Explore the possibilities. Open your mind and heart to the beauty of this world and its diverse people. You might surprise yourself by who you meet and how much you have in common. Plan on an unexpected good time. I am proud of you.

13

The next circle I added was a women's networking group that had met once a month for either an inspirational talk or a social activity. There was a nominal fee, but I was gain.

This will be my second year to have joined with these remarkable, courageous women. They have broken down barriers, fought hard for their dreams, and have made their mark in their fields of expertise. Most are business owners and entrepreneurs. They commit to supporting each other and uplifting each other's accomplishments. They motivate me.

When the monthly activity is a talk, the presenter is usually another woman of influence in our city and the topics range anywhere from personal health to career advancement to finance. I have learned so much already.

This women's networking group is another basket for me. I love it! Remember, going back to my pre-trauma days, I had friends from many different areas of life. I have even harkened back to high school to find 'that girl'. In high school, I ran track, I did the hurdles, high jump, and 550 relay. I was a majorette (which is a dancer/ baton twirler). I know, there's not many of us left today. I wrote for the school newspaper, I sang in the chorus, I was a member of the National Honor Society, I played in the annual powder puff football game, I was voted onto the student council where I served on different committees. I created, wrote and shared the afternoon announcements over the public announcement system. I went to a dancing school in the evenings and belonged to our youth group at our church. I had neighborhood friends, but mostly my friends came from my activities.

I know it might sound like I 'peaked' in high school. That is not what I am reflecting on here. What I *am* saying is that high school (for me personally) was a period of time before trauma. By resurrecting 'that girl', the real me comes back in direct proportion. In fact, THAT, my friend, is what I am going for. Not high school days themselves, but that innocent, (but wiser), I can do anything feeling I once had. This might be hard to relate to if you did not have a positive high school experience. Seek out your unique pre-trauma time. Hopefully, you get the idea. Share this self-discovery with one trusted person you know.

So, to return to pre-trauma Steph, or pre-trauma _____ (*your name*), let's keep building baskets and filling them. This women's networking group I described offers both professional AND social treasure. Bonus!! The social activities have included interesting classes like flower arranging, cooking, self-defense, and painting; a group Sound Bath, and even an evening dinner in a turt. Creativity, restoration, fun – always our intention on social nights!

2022 started out powerful with a goal planning workshop presented by one of our town's most dynamic women. It was fabulous! So many takeaways, so much to be excited for, so much to digest, apply and enjoy. We created personal vision statements, and value guides and even a 10-year narrative of our future life. It was fun and inspiring, raw and real. I really love these ladies. They are still new to me, but that in itself is part of the adventure.

The host was crazy amazing. She is a ballroom dancer and a triathlete who is also an Ironman. *Have you heard of that competition?* The contestants swim a TON of miles, bike a TON more and then finish with a run, like a 26K run/ marathon. Respect is an understatement.

Her company is called Moonshot XX. www.moonshotxx.com. From her website, Toni Hernandez is "an organizational culture trainer, executive leadership coach and champion for people development. She is a pitbull for the human experience." Well, she was every bit of that and more on our special night.

In my 10-year vision statement, I wrote of happy times, goals fulfilled and a well-ending legacy. My closing line was I have accomplished my mission. I *(with the help of God and love from precious people)* have created a legacy that loves and lasts and I have reversed generational brokenness. I set my intention for this vision and I pray it comes to pass. I see it. I believe.

I have always loved setting goals. I soak up that information at any seminar imaginable. We discuss goal setting deeper, later.

This radically candid, gracious woman also offered us a 30-minute complimentary private consultation. I will definitely take her up on that experience. I will help her to succeed any way I can too. For example, she has an exclusive once a month gathering for women to connect and be supportive of one another. It is a Mastermind so to speak. It is limited to 10 women and she puts out a discussion topic early. It seems like an excellent investment of time and resources. I will spread the word.

If you are looking for a soul to motivate you or your company, Toni Hernandez is your girl. Again, you can check out her website and connect at: www.moonshotxx.com.

Next month, our group is taking a self-defense class, Krav Maga specifically. I can't wait. Movement is important, much needed and a joy. I just love the mix of fun and education with these women and this group. I am thankful I found my way to them.

If you are not part of such a group, I recommend giving the idea consideration. Community is integral to healing. There are ways to connect no matter where you live. Try Meetup (www.meetup.com) per se. Their website is full of opportunities to connect to different groups of people based on common interest. Meetups are available almost everywhere. If you don't see a group you like, start one! How exciting is that, right?! Let me know how it goes.

As mentioned, most of the women in this networking group are entrepreneurs and I love to support them. Look at your sphere of influence and see how you can support them too. It will make you feel so good inside to pour into others. You can make it simple. Set aside a morning and text 5-10 people something encouraging and something you like about them uniquely. Reprograming your brain to give instead of waiting to receiving is healthy and healing. It will help balance your emotions and ground you. Do not think about if these texts are returned in any fashion. Just give! Wait and see, the rewards can be just in the composing and sending. You are rewiring your brain to see the good in people.

Next, set aside one day and make a phone call, perhaps two, dare I say three. You read that right – a phone call (s). Because of texting, I think we have gotten away from telephone conversations. I know texts are speedy and efficient, but sometimes I just miss the days of ringing family and friends. Let's bring calls back. They are more personal, you can have deeper exchanges, enjoy the sound of the person's voice and hear their tone too. There is less chance of misinterpretation as well. Leave a voicemail if you must; just a cheery greeting that you were thinking of them and wishing them well. One call a week at minimum. You can fit that in.

We are all busy. A trick I have incorporated in lately has been to schedule phone calls. I know that loses its spontaneity, but it works. While in a text conversation, I ask *"Would you like to catch up on the phone one day?"* They respond *"yes"* every time.

We then make an appointment. Yes, I make an actual appointment in my phone calendar, and I set the reminder notices. My phone allows me to invite them to add this appointment to their own phone calendar, so I do. I also put this appointment in my handwritten manual calendar in my kitchen. I enter the phone call times right alongside Dr. appointments and the like. I do color code these appointments by category. I know, that's a bit much. It's fun to me! I keep it simple. I draw a circle around the appointments with different colored highlighters. Pink for personal, yellow for Dr. appointments, and so on. This system helps keep me organized and as I glance at the month, I see connection sprinkled over the paper pages.

Longing for connection is innate, part of our condition, part of life. It is something we all share; whether everyone recognizes that need or not. If there is a 'no' when you reach out, understand that person may not be ready, or in the same place as you. It's not personal. Give them space. Try again if your heart leads you there. You are never wrong to reach out. Trust the timing of relationships to ebb and flow as they should, and be both grateful and anticipatory with the souls who cross your path. They are there for a purpose. Your path partner could be here for you, or you for them. We don't know, really. It is all Love.

14

Goals. I can't share enough about this topic. Over the years they have been horizons of hope for me, markers of progress or lack thereof, and avenues to bring about change.

As a family, we set annual goals. We recently started to review them quarterly; round about the start of each new season. This tradition helps keep us moving in the right direction. It's especially good for the children, I believe. The new goals are due New Year's Day or maybe the second. Our method: initial due date of 1/1, reviews approximately 3/20 (Spring), 6/21 (summer), 9/22 (fall), and 12/21 (winter). I take mine very seriously. I really do.

The family handwrites their individual goals and gives them to me. I type them up, give everyone a personal copy and post one on the refrigerator. The posting helps us stay on track. By setting the goal sheet before us in a highly seen place, we can more easily keep them in mind as we make daily decisions. Those decisions are the precursors for our habits. And you know, it's those habits, pesky or productive, that really determine the direction and ultimately the outcome of your life.

We divide up our goals into categories. We encourage spiritual, physical (health), relational, financial, and home improvement goals. Below is my list this year. Hold me accountable, please! Send me yours too if you want. The more you share and declare, the better chance they will come true.

Stephanie   2022

Prioritize relationship building

Read one book on marriage

Couples get-away

One date night per month

Pick up hobby with Kev (my husband xo)

Vacation with children

Be and maintain natural weight

Publish THAT girl

Have 12 book signings

Pilates weekly

Co-lead book club

Have all check-ups complete

The **home improvement goals** are plenty, and fun. It all depends on cashflow really. I try to make my goals realistic with a splash of dreamy. I would love an in-ground swimming pool, but I'll be happy with a new toilet installed. That may seem funny, but I have learned to be content. We live in a modest 2 bedroom, 1 bath home. Yes, you read that right. One bath! I really appreciate the other unique things about my home though. We live on 1.25 acres in an area zoned open rural – basically that means I can have chickens, even though I don't. We live minutes from town, and minutes from the beach. I'll take my one bath for the peace, quiet, of my semi-country living.

Physical / health goals are always on the list, year after year. They may change depending on age and personal progress, but they are present and a high priority. Did you notice my weight goal states to "be my natural weight"? Well, weight loss coach, author, and friend, Amy Suliano Cox, describes our natural weight as the weight we achieve when we know and listen to our body's cues and make consistent healthy choices. In short, Amy counsels that it is best to eat when we are hungry, (*really* hungry, not bored, angry or sad), stop when we are satisfied, (not stuffed, not uncomfortable), eat and drink whole foods that come from the earth not boxes or bags. Amy believes an occasional holiday treat is fun, and even important. She shares to follow this eating plan and move your body regularly in ways you enjoy and your body will heal itself of excess weight. If you want to know more or dig deeper, check out her website at: www.losethementalweight.com.

I also love this next **physical/ health** goal: have all checkups complete. For me, that means: dental, vision, ob/gyn, physical with blood work, and a mammogram or sonogram (I use HerScan). For an affordable way to get blood work done, check out: www.ultralalbtests.com. Order your labs online and pay at check out, then take your receipt to the lab of your choice to have your draw done. Well, my physician gave me this tip in our uninsured days.

You can even donate blood to get a VERY basic checkup. You will have your blood pressure and temperature taken before your donation. In a few weeks, you will receive an email with the cholesterol results from your donated blood. It will not break it down into HDL or LDL, but you can at least get your general cholesterol number. It's FREE! Sometimes, they will even pay you in form of a gift card etc. A nominal amount of course. $10 or so.

I guess the reason I emphasize the health goals because everything hinges on it. *Don't you think?* If I am suffering from a headache or back pain, I am definitely not as productive. In fact, I can be downright.... b*t*hy. I don't like feeling that way, I am sure you agree. So, the diet, supplementation, and exercise, (especially stretching) is at the core of all these goals. For in a healthy body, I can do the hard things.

As for **spiritual goals**, I think it is very individual. My faith is solid, but my faith *walk* goes from being super involved in a church community, to very intense alone time with my God; rarely somewhere in between. Take an inventory of your practices and see how and what works for you. Maybe my ebb and flows corelate to what is happening in my life. I tend to crave community when all is humming along nicely, I tend to seek answers from God alone when things are rough. I think the main reason could be the simple, 'how are you?' question that people ask in the foyer after a service. I say, 'fine', 'good' or the like when deep down my feelings are vacilating between sadness and gladness. I answer this way even when something very complicated is going on with myself or with a loved one. I feel hypocritical giving those pat answers, but I also understand it is not a healthy boundary to overshare with people who are not consistent in my life.

During those trying times, I retreat, I heal, then reengage. I have learned to keep things 'close to the vest' except for a few treasured people who I trust, who know my story, who will keep my confidence and who will tell me the truth, even when it's hard to hear. They are gold.

Although I may pull back publicly during certain seasons, I never stop deepening my faith on a personal and private level. I also try to incorporate a sabbath, a day of rest, one day a week. Some like to observe a specific day and stick to a rigid schedule, me any day works where I can carve out a major chunk of time to be quiet, reflective and still.

As for **financial goals**, well, I try not to overcomplicate this matter. My husband and I are hard workers, we are wise spenders, and we save a small portion of our income. We are focusing on being debt free before we increase our amount of savings. Sure, I'd like to be further ahead, but we take two vacations a year and have one date a month. The vacations may be bare bones, but we take them. Our dates may be sparse, but we enjoy them. My point is that some advisors teach zero fun until you are debt free. ZERO. That philosophy, and I speak from experience, does not work for me. Tried, and tried, the all-hands-on debt plan, but I realized I need more balance. Do what's best for you and your situation. There are many angles to approach the same end game. And since each of our end game desires are different, so can be our strategies.

Lastly, and ultimately, the most important of goals: **relationship goals**. This year, I summarized my relationship goals as a desire to prioritize my people. I often poured so much energy into situations and into those who tug on my heart for one reason or another that I would have nothing left for myself or my immediate family. I identify as a bit of an empath. Not entirely, but in some ways. Example, after I serve or spend time with someone hurting, I tend to think about them often after we part. So, when I set the goal to prioritize relationships, my heart means to continue to love on others, but when I get home, emotionally disconnect and be present with my husband, children, pets and myself. I am learning to shift gears and refocus on home and my surroundings.

You may need or want to achieve this mindfulness too. Leaving behind work is equally necessary for your well-being. Brainstorm here. *What are ways that you can change states in a healthy fashion? How can you compartmentalize work from, home?* This separation can be even more difficult now that so many have remote / work from home jobs. For these workers, no longer can the commute home be a time of transition.

I think this unwinding, this mental switch, should be unique to all. No exceptions. It depends on how you are wired, the health of your nervous system, your living situation, and the stress level of your occupation.

Let's establish that alcohol cannot be your choice. I know, it's an easy go-to, but it will only make your nervous system worse in the long run. So, exercise, do meditation, take a bath or shower, go for a walk, spend time with a pet, sing, read, sit outdoors and watch the sunset; or whatever activity centers you and evokes joy. Commit to this transition time to regroup, find peace and bring balance to your emotions.

Once you transition from service or work, it will be easier to be present, be attentive and be a source of calm for your home. Whether you live alone or with family, practicing this shifting is important. It will bring about a healthier you who will make healthier choices and your life will be a display of these decisions.

Start small. Do the shift just one day a week, then move up to two days until you do this every day you are working in any capacity away from home. Shifting will soon become second nature, a good habit, a blessing.

We've discussed all kinds of goals: physical/health, spiritual, financial, relational and even home improvement. There could be categories I have not mentioned. Throw out all your ideas; your dreams and visions. Break them into your categories, commit to which ones you feel led to accomplish each year. They will change from season to season too. What I wanted in my 20s is sure different than today's goals and I know that they will continue to evolve, as they should.

Finding an accountability partner also helps keep you on track. Accountability partners certainly do not have to be family, just a person who will hold your feet to the fire, and be passionate about your success.

If you currently don't have a set of goals, pause here. Grab that notebook and write down 12 goals. Yes, right now. And YES – 12. *Be quick. Don't overthink. Let it flow from within, from your gut, from your spirit, from that still small voice. GO!*

List: 3 – physical/ health, 3 – relational, 3-spiritual, 3-financial. There are your 12 goals. You did it!

Now, post them where you can see them every day. Read them aloud when you can. You have goals now. You have direction. You create your life by your choices. Choose well. I'm proud of you!!

15

We talked a good deal about circle changing, or at least evaluated our sphere of influence. *How about circle keeping?* Yes, there is such incredible value in spending quality time with friends that knew you 'when'. 'When' there was no drama, no trauma and no scars (or just a few). Hang out with them some and see. They'll remember things you don't and help you uncover 'that girl'.

I have had a few events over the last several years that started my process of rediscovering 'that girl'. It was basic, beautiful, and fun. The anticipation of these events was part of the excitement for sure. It all started with my 35th class reunion in Pittsburgh, Pennsylvania. We were going. My husband, daughter (12) and me. My son was grown and living large in another state.

The reunion fell over two days. Day one consisted of taking in a baseball game. We were traveling from Florida by car to the reunion so we did not make it in for that particular night. A sporting event was perfect though! If you know Pittsburghers, we love our teams!! Black and gold, terrible towels, the works. We made it in town late Friday afternoon.

Since we would miss the baseball game, I had set up a mini-reunion and dinner with my dad's side of the family. We had to eat, right? Why not eat with a purpose and intention. Rakoci (formerly Rakoczy) was my paternal family's surname. The mini-reunion turned out better than I imagined.

Planning the event was so much fun. I picked a restaurant that was centrally located near where most of my relatives lived. The restaurant had a separate area for groups and they could also serve buffet style. The best part is that they served our traditional food: halupki (which is stuffed cabbage), haluski (which is wide dumpling type noodles with buttered cabbage and onions), kielbasa, and pierogies – OF COURSE! Polka music in the background was the perfect touch. We had some takers on the carved-out dance floor, most were under the age of 12, but none the less people were dancing.

That family reunion day was very special to me. Worth the drive, every mile. I would have travelled just for this affair. It was so wonderful to see so many kin. I even made the rounds about the room, interviewing everyone as to their branch of our family tree. Unprepared, I took the paper placemats from the tables to record the information. I HAD to know. Thinking back now, I should have brought a huge poster board to draw the tree on. *Next time!*

Never, ever would I have imagined that in the midst of this very chapter as I write about my ethnicity and family gathering, Ukrainians are bravely fighting for their freedom, land and very lives. Yes, I am 50% Ukrainian. My father was 100% Ukrainian. My grandparents lived in what is now (today) Lviv, Ukraine. That makes my nationality Ukrainian and my ethnicity East Slavic.

You see, my dad was the baby of twelve children. I believe that number is correct. I'm not sure, though. My grandparents emigrated through Poland to the US. I have a picture taken in the 'old country' of my grandparents with four other adults. The photo was taken before their emigration. We do not know who the other adults are in the picture, but we are guessing that they are their brothers and sisters. We don't know them so we believe they stayed behind in the Ukraine so there is a real possibility of blood relatives there. My heart is breaking, as I am sure yours is over the situation.

Today is 3/4/2022. It is in the heat of the battle. I don't know where this conflict is headed. I admit I am scared at times. I can't let it consume me. I must go about living my life. I try to shield my daughter as I am able. I can't process the news myself most of the time. How could she or even why should she? It's a hard balance to stay informed without letting the fear and worry seep in, or stay.

Part of finding 'that girl' is exploring our heritage and ethnicity. I am learning new things about my background these days in an unexpected place – the world stage. Brave, determined, principled – I see such characteristics in those citizens and I can see the same characteristics in me and my tree, both roots and branches. *What about you? Where are your ancestors from? What can you find out?*

I am a little skeptical about the DNA programs you see offered on TV. Just like my fingerprints, etc., I just don't want an entity to have my DNA. I would LOVE to know the results, don't get me wrong, but I am on the fence about the actual procedure. However, I have heard so many heartwarming, success stories from those programs, it just might be worth the gamble. To find a long lost loved one or to meet a relative you never knew existed must be a miraculous experience. If you have one of those stories, please do share with me.

I love the family tree component to figuring out what makes us tick. I guess I am quite curious how and why traits, good or bad, are passed down from one generation to another. Whether genetically, epigenetically, or simply habit, everyone up the line had a hand in who you are today. Embrace it all. Enjoy your unique make-up. Keep trying to make a positive difference in your own life, and your legacy.

I feel pressed to add something here. I want to share what's on my heart for you in this present moment. There is so much going on in the world. It's time to ramp up any self-care and stress management techniques you have at your fingertips to process the happenings without losing hope.

Gratitude helps me the most when I feel I am in a sinking ship. By day, I look around and name all my blessings in sight. Or if it's night, in bed, when all are asleep, except me, I will list my blessings one by one until I drift back off to sleep. Thankfulness can stop the spiral down for most. If it doesn't, reach out for help either personally or professionally. Don't go it alone when you feel the water rising. Tomorrow is a new day, full of possibilities. There will be light. Give it a chance.

16

I'll circle back now to my class reunion which is why we headed to Pittsburgh that fall. The reunion was held in the small suburb of Elrama, PA at a local Gun Club. Now, you might find that a strange choice, but it was really ideal. It had lots of land, picnic shelters and a bonfire area. We are a down to earth bunch so this set-up was perfect.

A good friend and I went shopping weeks before for just the right outfit. I got a button up soft light-colored denim dress, short sleeved and mid-thigh length. It was cute. I did a last-minute push to lose weight before the event. It worked and I can say I kept a good portion of the weight off. Not all, but some. My silly secret (most nutritionists would not recommend) was that I did the infamous cabbage soup diet about two weeks before the trip. For the most part, I was already eating sensibly so the cabbage soup diet was just for good measure. The trick here is that I actually LOVE, love, love the cabbage soup recipe itself so it does not feel like a sacrifice for me. It is so yummy! I also got my hair colored (roots and foil), and my nails done too. A mani/ pedi in a neutral color, gel on my fingernails. An eyebrow wax, and I was ready.

It was so much fun! It was covered dish and a small fee to cover the rental of the club. I can't remember the food hardly, just the experience of seeing people from long ago. A few friends who also came from far away stayed in our hotel. They surprised me with a knock at my hotel door early that morning to say hello! It was a blast! I was tired at that early morning hour, but I was so happy to see them!! They were actually two friends who I had been fortunate enough to see over the years. That's one of the very cool things about living in Florida. It seems that everyone comes down here at one point or another. Beach vacation, taking kids to Disney or to see Grandma and Grandpa. I'm so glad that I had been able to see these ladies fairly often and that we have kept in touch. It felt like yesterday!

I had packed my senior yearbook. We dug it out right away and started leafing through the glossy pages. We were giggling and talking over each other as we each shared our take down memory lane. Girls are gifted in this bubbling over communication style, aren't we? Since this was my first high school reunion, I am sure my excitement was greater than most.

If my memory serves me correctly, the reunion started at 3pm so there was time in the morning to do some things about town, and besides I was already wide awake from my friends' visit to our hotel room. My husband, Kevin, daughter, who was then 13, and I went on a short hometown tour. We crossed over the river into the town of Elizabeth. There I showed them the places I lived, the playground I played on, where I stood from the freezing winter wind when I was a patrol / crossing guard for my school. They saw my elementary school (which sadly is closed now). They saw where I shopped, they saw where I got my hair done, our family car fixed, and where I took my dance lessons. They saw my family home that I grew up in after my dad won custody of me my 7th grade summer. (That story could be a book itself). They even met a couple of neighbors on my street. It was such a good, good feeling to see these familiar places and people. Why did I wait so long?

By 1pm, we returned to the hotel where we got ready for the reunion. I wasn't sure if any other children would be attending. It turned out that my daughter was among three. I am glad she was there.

We arrived right on time. The weather was warm, but would grow chilly by nightfall. We checked in, then meandered our way to the buffet where we placed our dish to share. I recognized face after face. It was a special evening full of hugging, reminiscing, and laughter.

Later, we made a plan. Well, one of my dear friends made a plan, a suggestion that was so exciting. How about a girls' trip? YES! Unanimously, friends chimed in with interest. I piped up that I would host being from the sunshine state and all. I really was hyped now.

We have had two girls' trips since that reunion and I can't wait for the next one. *Have you ever taken a girls' trip with high school or college friends? Or perhaps neighbors or co-workers you were once or are now close to?* I highly recommend this sort of thing and I will share more in a coming chapter on how to make this happen.

If you were one of thousands that high school wasn't your vibe, don't get stuck here. Skip your reunions if that feels right to you. But perhaps try. People mature. If it's safe, reconcile and make peace with your past and your people. They do not need to come into your future, but their roles in your life will help piece together 'that girl'.

If you were bullied (or if you were a bully), the consequences are painful and long-lasting. I had two incidents where I was bullied in school; once in middle school (8th grade art class to be precise), and high school (10th grade- hall, lunch, bus, bathroom...same bully, different locations). I look back now with a new set of eyes. I want to send love to that little girl (me/ my inner child) and I also want to extend compassion to my two bullies.

I share this part of my story so you know that I understand bullying firsthand and that my compassion runs deep for all who lived it.

I think the adage is true that bullied people bully. Report it at once to the appropriate channels so that the situation can be addressed and stopped. The cycle perpetuates so the sooner, the better.

Once you are healed, consider advocating to stop bullying in your community. Speak out, tell your story and you could be changing or even saving a life. It may be painful to retell your experience, but being vulnerable and sharing your pain could be the catalyst that prompts a bully to stop their action.

Consider forgiving that person or persons as it is only hurting *you* each day, as bitterness grows little by little. I mostly mean forgiving in your heart, not in person which is often not possible, or prudent. Forgiveness frees. I know it might be impossible to forget, but once you have more positive experiences in your life, it will be easier to move past the memories. Helping others can ease that burden too and even turn it into a purpose. Explore that idea and journal about it. Pen a letter to 'that girl'.

17

From my high school reunion sparked a new and special tradition. A girls' only trip! A friend suggested the idea, and I offered to take the lead. Being a Florida resident, I thought it would be fun and easy. It turned out to be such a joy to plan and attend. We have two in the books now; and a third in the works.

You can do this with just one girl friend or dozens. The RSVPs have varied from year to year. A large invite went out each trip with attendance increasing every time. I created the invitation through Evite which is an online invitation platform. www.evite.com. It was a simple, free and convenient way to keep track of replies and other communication. I started out inviting a core group of women, my besties if you will, and then encouraged them

to send me contact info on any girl they would like to invite. The guest list was long and is still growing today.

Everyone is in different seasons of life so this tradition might not work for all in the moment, but one year it will be right so keep sending those invitations. It seems most possible for empty nesters, but I think everyone could use this time away at any season if their circumstances permit. Think outside the box. Travel far for a destination getaway or do a staycation in your hometown. Either way, plan. Get it on the books. Calendar it.

Just having it out there in the future will lift your spirits daily. Really.

I'll tell you how I put ours together so you can use it as a guide. First, I picked a weekend. I chose the same weekend as the weekend our high school reunion fell on because the class officers conducted a survey and that weekend won hands down. I figured if it was good one year, it would also be good the next. It was late September, the 9/23-9/25 weekend, to be exact.

I decided to host in my hometown for the first girls' trip because I would know it best and I wanted it to go smoothly and be a blast. I chose an oceanfront Five Diamond resort just minutes from my home and about 30 miles from our airport. Now, before you check out, thinking the accommodations are unaffordable, remember…. you are sharing the costs. I figured the home base per se, the hotel had to be top notch, clean, on the water, and have impeccable service. It exceeded expectations.

Since most ladies did not live near the ocean, and they would be traveling far, I wanted them to have an experience that would be worth the distance, time and money. So, I don't lose you here. It is doable. I even paid my room off in advance. Just a little every month, so that when the weekend came, the only money I needed was food and drinks. (And that bill too was small as we entertained out of our rooms or in the common areas of the resort.)

Let's talk real numbers. A room or suite with tax and resort fees that would accommodate 3-4 girls is going to run about $400 per night. $400 multiplied by 3 nights divided by 4 guests equal $300. SO, for one gal to spend 3 nights at a Five Diamond resort would be $300 total plus food and drinks. $300 divided by 12 months (one year of preparation) equals $25 per month. Of course, travel is extra. But, just think… a long weekend at a 5-Diamond resort for $25 per month. You can do that!!

Travel. Book ahead, drive, carpool, just get there. I did not plan my friends' transportation or arrivals or departures. They handled that on their own and they did so marvelously.

Grab your yearbook, start to turn those pages and reminisce. Have a pad nearby and jot down the names of those gals that were dear to you back then. Maybe go one circle out. Be brave. Go two circles out. By circle, I mean layers of friendships.

Example: inner circle – 'besties', next circle – a girl in your class who was more of an acquaintance than friend, but perhaps you went to her birthday parties in grade school. Or a girl you may have drifted apart from in high school, but you were once close with in elementary or middle school. Next circle – girls from your neighborhood or bus or a sports team. You may not know them too well, but they were in your proximity. And finally, everyone who RSVP's yes, be sure to ask them if there is any girl they would like to invite, and include them. That should make a well-rounded, inclusive group.

I believe one of the positives from the 2019+ pandemic was the use of Zoom. I mean, I had hardly ever used the platform before that year. But, WOW! Connection was possible again. Of course, Zoom was not as special as in-person connections, but it felt good. *Didn't it?* I know people are probably tired of Zoom by now, but what a blessing it was for many. I mention Zoom because I think that is a good place to hold a kickoff event to discuss the getaway.

My tips to the host here are: 1) Make your guest list. 2) Get their contact information. 3) Create the Evite. Choose a design that matches the destination. 4) Send out the Evite. 5) Send out the

Zoom link to the whole guest list, or at least to the yes and maybe RSVPs. 6) Have a general trip agenda planned and ready to present. Get feedback, be flexible, but share more than solicit.

The excitement builds when everyone sees each other on Zoom. If your getaway is fun and affordable with lots of advance notice, people will make their best effort to join. Reach out and share your trip pics and memories with me. I am so proud of you!!

18

Personal development, you could say, has become a hobby of mine. I enjoy learning about human behavior, positive psychology and definitely neuroplasticity. The idea that we have the ability to form new paths and thought patterns in our brains is nothing short of amazing to me. This miracle makes me feel like I am born again, with a whole new chance at living large.

Interesting that I am just now, at age 57, finding out how the mind works, but I am grateful to be here. No matter your age, you can begin again. It takes work, lots of consistent, disciplined work, but it's worth it. Think of the possibilities in life and love when we have cleaned out the cobwebs of regret and shame, and have embraced the future with compassion and confidence.

I appreciate all I have gone through; I have asked forgiveness from those I have hurt along the way. I have forgiven myself. Whenever pain from the past creeps into my thinking, I pause, reframe, and imagine the person I am today comforting me in that former place when I was lost and broken. I am filled with self-compassion rather than guilt. I am filled with love for myself in all the stages these years have presented. I can't change the past. And I invite you and those around me to accept this truth too.

To be clear, I am not condoning my poor choices, I am just recognizing that by letting them go, and covering them with self-compassion and love, I can better serve my God, myself and others. As time marches on, I have learned to accept myself, even the not so pretty parts that just flat out feel part of my DNA. I have worked hard on these shadowy parts though and I believe I can become the best version of myself in my lifetime. I will keep moving forward, one day at a time, hoping to master my growth as destined. I will call upon my God and my fellow sojourners for help, and I am ready to help you too.

I am curious, and I am more courageous than ever. Fear of others' opinions are no longer a factor in my life. People-pleasing is out the door too for the most part. I will continue to love and care for those who want to be recipients of my love, but the rest can be on their merry way. Naysayers are not my people. Saying good-bye was complex, although the majority weren't in-person actual goodbyes. They just took place in my heart. They were boundaries. Long overdue boundaries, really. I only had to announce the hard line to a few. I am incredibly grateful for the knowledge I have gained over these past years that made me brave enough to make good on this conviction.

My nervous system is still a work in progress. Trauma is an embodied experience living in your innermost parts. I am calmer and more settled now than at any other point in my life and I am grateful. Self-care is my number one priority and this equates to the best overflow for my family, friends and community. What I used to consider selfish pursuits; I now know as love. Simply love.

I start my day early. I am working on adjusting my circadian rhythm to come closer to the sun's hours. Circadian rhythm is defined by Wikipedia as a natural, internal process that regulates the sleep-wake cycle and repeats roughly every 24 hours. Yes, that's what I'm aiming to adjust.

Summering in Maine helps the process. My husband's family owns a home there that we are blessed to reside in during each July. The sun rises there over the beautiful lake by 5:00am, sometimes even earlier. The sun sets around 9pm and it stays light until at least 9:30pm. Bright, gorgeous days make mind-blowing starry nights. It is an ideal season and place to reset your sleep schedule. But, don't let location stop you. The idea is to be awake during daylight, wind down as it gets dark, sleep between 7-9 hours or whatever your body requires to thrive. You can recalibrate any season, and anywhere. Enjoy!

Here are the specifics of my routine. I use my iPhone to aid me. I set my bedtime at 10pm and my wake-up time at 6am. A reminder chimes at 9pm to start my 'wind down'. This means a slow, methodical bedtime routine. It means a lot to me.

I usually take a warm to hot bath around 8:30pm. I soak for 20 minutes or more with Epsom Salts; sometimes adding a little baking soda too. While the bath water is running, I dry brush my skin in upward motions to improve circulation, open my pores, and prepare my body to detox from the day. I light a soy candle or enjoy our beautiful flameless ones. Then, I pull up my Spotify and play either a relaxing, spa-like instrumental song or perhaps a guided meditation. I relax and shift gears. My meditation choice is one that engages visualization, or some sort of forward thinking. I would not want to fall asleep in the bathtub. Be careful. If falling asleep in the bathtub concerns you, please set a timer or tell a member of your household, and definitely leave the door unlocked. I, personally, do not use guided meditation to sleep. I deep breathe into my slumber.

Taking a warm bath, of course, raises your body temperature. Once you are out, your body works to cool itself down which signals sleep. I love comfy jammies! Flowery, cozy, anything that makes me feel relaxed and beautiful. (Sexy too for the right occasion xo)

After bath, I dry off gently with a fresh towel, the fluffier the better. I use a non-toxic lotion to moisturize my body, and brush out my hair if I shampooed. My favorite brush doubles as a scalp massager. This particular brush does an outstanding job! It stimulates the hair follicles which encourages growth, moves residual stress away, and just feels so good. I have seen firsthand stronger and thicker hair. Don't skip this step. If you are looking for a quality brush like this one, write me and I will send you the link to order.

Next, I brush and floss my teeth, followed by mouthwash and a tongue scraping. Ahh! Dental hygiene is so important.

The last step to my regimen is to moisturize my face, neck and decolletage. I change up my anti-aging products all the time so I really do not endorse any one product line. I do massage my face while applying the cream in an upward motion, sort of following the new sculpting trend. I think it is working! Even if the resurrected cheek bones are just my imagination, the technique sure feels good!

After I leave the bathroom, I stop using my phone for the night. I am not a big TV watcher so this is a non-issue for me. Next, I set up my bedroom diffuser. I use high-end lavender. This is my only essential oil I use so I did splurge here. I don't use the color changing light feature on the diffuser at night; sometimes during the day if I just want to take a 'time out' in my bedroom. While it begins to churn, I look around and do a final tidy of the bedroom and turn down the sheets – hotel style. What a treat! I LOVE fresh, clean sheets. I launder them at least once per week.

At this point, I do a few stretches before turning in. Nothing too strenuous, just a little movement to work out any excess energy in my body. I then put a few drops of my lavender essential oil on my wrist and rub them together, then one tiny drop behind each ear. That should do it!

Next, I turn off my bedside lamp and get in bed. I have four beautiful flameless decorated candles; each at a different height. They are displayed on my chest of drawers on a dainty lace doily. The candles are on a timer for five hours. They turn on at 6pm and turn off at 11pm, giving off just the right amount of soft light in the room.

Once in bed, I relax, let my mind sort of float trying not to focus on any one topic. If I don't drift right to sleep, I do some deep breathing. *Try this*: breathe in 5 counts, hold 5 counts, breathe out 5 counts, pause 5 counts, repeat.

A new concept I just learned of is called sleep drive. Basically, it is your *need* for sleep. If you have a healthy sleep drive, it will be easier to fall asleep and ultimately stay asleep. By following a circadian rhythm that aligns with the sun rise and sun set, resisting the urge to nap, and getting moderate exercise, your sleep drive should improve. When your body and mind *need* sleep, your slumber may be deeper and include multiple REM and dream stages that will allow your body to restore itself overnight.

And as an added bonus, if you are sober or sober curious, these tips may help you not look to alcohol as a sleep aid. It really does work. Try it. And let me know.

Once you start to feel the benefits of good sleep, you will fight for it. It will become a necessity you just can't negotiate with any longer. Funny, I remember my parents insisting on a bedtime. As a teen, you don't understand or want to comply, but I am thankful today for that early discipline. It's not too late for you to embrace the day, and night too!

19

Cognitive dissonance. When I first saw this term again recently, I was brought back to my Psychology class in high school. I couldn't pin down the meaning yet in my mind, but it rang a bell for sure. As soon as I read the definition, an alarm went off. Not just in my brain, but in my spirit. Cognitive dissonance was my lived experienced for so long. Although I had become THAT GIRL in most areas, I was not living life full out yet. There was still a nagging duality of some kind going on inside me. Not always, but sometimes. Now, I was relieved to know there was a formal name to my plight.

For a long time, at least years, I have had a 'check' in my spirit to make some changes, both internally and physically. When you have this crisis of conscience and you continually shut down that 'voice', the voice only gets louder and these two conflicting 'lives' only seem to clash more.

So, this search for and reclaiming of 'that girl' has been a long time coming. It has been simmering and even boiling over from time to time. This match now between who I am and who I was pre-trauma settles the cognitive dissonance and that alignment brings me peace.

I recently just experienced this 'match' most profoundly in a religious service. Lots of things were happening at the moment. I was singing when the feeling came to me.

First, singing out loud I learned stimulates your Vagus nerves which are said to activate your parasympathetic nervous system responsible for 'calmness'. Let me summarize what I learned about this subject. Most, if not all, this knowledge came from the Sounds True Trauma Skills Summit that I attended virtually awhile back. It is the workshop that I shared about in an earlier chapter. I am so grateful for the scholarship I received granting me lifetime access to the Summit in the digital library the organization offers its members. I learned from some of the best like: Deb Dana and also Stephen Porges who introduced the Polyvagal Theory in 1994.

From my limited understanding, the parasympathetic nervous system reverses or 'puts out the fire' from the sympathetic nervous system. 'Puts out the fire' is also known as the 'fight or flight response.' This 'fight or flight response' is commonly activated in moments of sudden or great stress. If you have experienced a lot of traumas in your life as I had, your 'fight or flight' mode can stay stuck on so to speak making it difficult to calm your body and mind, doing damage to organs and hormones.

I learned from these experts that singing is a way to stimulate the Vagus nerves which is one of the reasons it is enjoyable and healing. I am not a scientist, or anything close, but I do know that I have always LOVED singing; especially in church, and now I know why. This explanation is divine and supernatural to me. It just amazes me that we were created to calm ourselves in this manner. SO, belt it out! Sing your heart out and feel the good vibrations!

Back to cognitive dissonance, this goes a bit deep and is super personal. You may or may not have such experiences so do not compare your healing to mine, or to anyone's, really. But the joy I felt singing that Sunday was different than I had ever quite experienced in my life.

You see, it had been pressed upon me for a while now to cut back or cut out drinking alcohol. For the longest time, I didn't listen to that 'still, small voice' inside me. I was determined to keep squashing that feeling and silencing that voice. Let me also say here that this was a personal impression on *my* spirit to make this change, and it is not meant in any way to suggest this is a path you must take too. You listen to your own 'voice', conscience, God. My point here is that it is important, even imperative to balance that cognitive dissonance by listening to *your* 'still, small voice' no matter what name you give it. (Universe, Holy Spirit, the Divine, ……). I believe, that once you dial in and fine tune 'the voice', you will receive instructions and the sooner you follow these instructions, the sooner your healing will come.

My 'voice' was telling me to slow down my drinking, and if I listened closer, I believe it was telling me to quit. If you are the type of person who thinks of God (or your name of choosing) as a loving parent, then you would believe that voice to have your best interest in mind. If you are a parent yourself, then you know that your heart aches if you see your child making choices that are not good for their health or well-being.

You might even say "If only they would listen to my advice...." "If only they would do what I suggest......"

Well, that was my dilemma, my quandary, the place where I got stuck emotionally and physically. I felt like I was supposed to stop drinking, but instead of listening to that hunch, instead of changing direction, I just kept on doing the same thing over and over. It did not matter that I did not technically fall into the category of alcohol use disorder. It mattered that I went my own way. The plunging forward and my refusal to make a change was what was causing me emotional havoc.

The tug and pull of knowing what you are supposed to do while doing the opposite to me is the ultimate cognitive dissonance. And being in church, particularly during the singing, or worship, portion of the service is when my pain of confliction was greatest.

Early July 2022, while summering in Maine, I attended our lake church as I usually do while in town. It's a small church, with modest amenities, compared to the megachurches of the south. This is part of its appeal to me. I prefer a church, building and all, but that's just my preference. It's partially due to being raised that way and that it brings me warm and safe feelings sitting quietly in a service. I also believe in community and for the most part I have found a sense of belonging in a body of seekers. There definitely were some painful experiences in church circles in the past, but overall, over the course of 57 years, I can say I have loved my faith and my spiritual practice.

This one particular Sunday, I noticed something missing inside me. That visceral pain had left. That nagging, jabbing feeling was replaced with peace. My values and my actions were matching and the cognitive dissonance had all but disappeared. I was just over 30 days alcohol-free. That's right, *free*.

Freedom is the best word I could use to describe that day. Symbolically, it was like the knife that was stabbing me for years was suddenly removed. The pain was gone. The dull ache was now barely noticeable as the healing of that wound began. To be right with your 'maker', to not fight against yourself, or war against your own conscience, is a place where peace meets reality. The pressure, the nudging gone. Just like that.

The final piece was in place. It fit. I am 'that girl', unbroken. No longer fragmented in different parts. No longer is there a disconnect between my values and my choices. What I believe and who I am is the SAME. I am whole. I am who I was created to be. Free. Free to dream, free to live and love, free to be *me*.

An even deeper understanding of this process came to me recently. I was again visiting Maine. It was fall 2022. My Pastor there at The Deeper Well Church, Mark Wheeler, shared his thoughts about what he coined soul trauma. He explained that where there is trauma, there is also a behavior that a person uses to offset or cope with the pain of that trauma. (In church culture, that behavior is called sin.) Pastor Mark also shared that this behavior blocks God and consequentially our healing because God cannot commune with sin. Once we do the work and remove the behavior, our connection to God is restored and we are restored.

Pastor Mark is currently working on a book of his own based on his remarkable life story. To hear his messages or find out about Pastor Mark's book release, you may follow him on Facebook and YouTube.

I also realized that this transformation, this newness of consciousness, this awakening of cohesiveness between who I wanted to be, and who I was in that moment was very, very personal. Although it happened in a church service, I believe this profound healing can happen anywhere. Be open. I know you are ready. Receive. I am proud of you!

20

It would be remiss of me not to share my journey in its entirety. My return to 'that girl' happened in layers. I hope you learn from them all. I reserved this change for last as I know it may come with resistance. It may or may not be for you. I will present it the same.

As I touched on in the last chapter, I have recently (the last 12 months or so) decided to take a look at my alcohol intake and habits. It has been an eye opening and a necessity to explore. I invite you to do the same.

[INSERT: Let's pause here. Today is Nov 1, 2022. I am in the midst of the final edit of this book. This section in particular is very personal. I

am going to intentionally leave the dates and present tense in to bring home the point that progress takes time. Years in fact as you will see. Think of it more as a peek into my journal or diary. If these "entries" seem confusing at times, stay with me. They reflected my understanding of the subject at the moment. The way we change is very individual to each of us, but I believe this aspect is especially unique. Our paths may be similar, or not at all. That's ok. You determine the direction. I have come to realize that growth doesn't stop unless YOU stop it. Keep going friends. Master resilience. You are stronger than you know.)

In early January 2022, I noticed a trend called Dry January. I am well dug into my mindful drinking journey at this time. I started actually in July 2021 and I have zero regrets. I realized during that summer that happy hour had become a given, a daily habit. Summer for us in Maine was a glorious experience and to "celebrate" regularly was part of the magic; until it wasn't.

Each afternoon in Maine, as a family, we headed to our lakeside dock at 3 or 4pm, cooler in hand, filled with adult beverages. And maybe a juice box, or two. So fun, but there was a nagging. I knew that hour was early, too early, for me anyway. I wanted to be fully present for this amazing time of year. I really did. I mean floating in my inflatable tube in a crystal-clear lake surrounded by mountains was nothing short of awe striking. Worth being present for, no question. But day. after sunny day, I indulged.

That was when my google search for help landed me on a miraculous app called: Reframe. I started this app and its program in July 2021. I was learning so much and looked forward to learning even more as time went on. I started to question why "celebrate" always included alcohol. I know I am not alone with this question.

Now, this step in my healing, the step of rethinking alcohol's role in my life, may not be important to you personally, but perhaps my experience may nudge you enough to consider the relationship just the same.

All of this time I have focused on food and seeing it as a toxin or fuel. It never dawned on me to think of my beverages, adult or otherwise as food, per say. All that has now changed. When I began to learn and understand that alcohol is a poison that your body must remove, I began to reconsider its appeal.

Once I realized this information, all things drinking changed. More like, once I stopped ignoring this information, the change began, gradually, and with lots of setbacks. I was a beer drinker. I loved the cold, crisp beverage. It was refreshing and calming to me. I liked it, but I knew it did not like me. As Marie Kondo says, "The best way to find out what we really need is to get rid of what we don't."

To be upfront, it has taken me almost a whole year to go alcohol-free. I tried moderation. I tried experimenting with different kinds of alcohol, even "healthy" wines or other liquors that supposedly have helpful ingredients. Ultimately, I realized I needed to change tracks from cut back to cut out.

As of 7/5/2022, I am 25 days alcohol-free. It is best for me, my body, and my mind. I have already experienced so many positive improvements; I don't plan to turn back. I will share more hurdles and highlights I experience along the way. I expect a lot of both. For now, I am enjoying this choice and hope to embrace it for life. And interestingly, when I was 'that girl' (pre-trauma), I did not drink. *Is being sober and being 'that girl' just a coincidence or is it critical?* Either way, I am resolved.

I use the Reframe app daily. I am learning about alcohol's toxicity, and its impact on our bodies. I am learning about how it effects our health both physically and mentally; and how it effects our relationships with ourselves and others. You can choose either a cut back or cut out track. I started out on the cut back track. On June 11. 2022, I changed from cut back to quit. The app is amazing filled with activities, goals and tools, courses, workshops and meetings. It offers places to journal, to track mood, stress, and even your appetite. There is a forum and opportunities to participate in community.

I downloaded the app July 17, 2021, and ironically my one month sober will fall almost one year to the day of that download. It is an excellent resource and an affordable place to see if this journey would help you reach your goals. Even if you are just curious, I highly recommend Reframe.

Although the monthly Reframe membership fee is nominal, there is a FREE app called "I am Sober". The free version is basic, but upgrades are available at cost. After having gone through the Reframe program almost three times in the past year, I have now transitioned to this "I am Sober" app. It tracks my days, allows me to make a daily pledge, then review the results of the day with room for feedback. All this to say, do not let lack of money deter you from starting an alcohol conscious life.

I could not end this chapter without acknowledging Dr. Brooke Scheller. I came across her practice on Instagram. Funny, sometimes, how serendipitous life can be. Having already been introduced to functional medicine through Dr. Kristy Harvell, my belief and interest in these approaches to health were my comfort zone. I recognized Dr. Brooke also from Reframe where she would lead workshops on nutrition for sobriety. Her teachings resonated with me more than any other method or strategy. Her specialty is using nutrition and functional medicine to change a person's relationship with alcohol.

She coined the term, "Functional Sobriety" and started her own online community called "Functional Sobriety Network" as well as an in-depth, self-paced training course called "The Functional Sobriety Academy." I became a

Founding Member of this supportive community (FSN) in June 2022; just days after my quit date of June 11, 2022. It was her expertise that helped me get where I am today.

Under Dr. Brooke's care, my health markers have improved dramatically. My blood pressure has dropped to an average of 117/76. My resting heart rate now averages 55 bpm. (Prior to working with Dr. Brooke, my blood pressure averaged 148/95 and my resting heart rate stayed around 98 bpm). I have lost 28 lbs. total since 1/1/22; 18 lbs. while working with Dr. Scheller.

There is no price tag I can put on these improvements in my health. The change has given me a new lease on life. Plugging away at dieting was not working. Trying to quit drinking with sheer willpower was not working. I needed more. There was a missing link.

It was Dr. Scheller's approach that changed everything for me. Her custom nutrition and supplementation plan made all the difference in my body and brain. I wanted to stay alcohol-free, I wanted to lose weight, I wanted to feel better, sleep better, live and love better. It took a little time, but I am hitting all these goals. My toolbox is finally full.

Fast forward. Today, I sit here writing in my local library. It is a Saturday. It is day 111 days alcohol-free for me. My birthday is in a few days. This one is special, different. There is so much extra to celebrate this year. Mostly, freedom.

You see, my mind used to constantly mull over thoughts of *"I need to lose weight. I need to quit drinking."* Not anymore. Those thoughts are gone, along with many other negative thoughts. Without these persistent thoughts, my mind is free. **FREEE!** I can think and dream *and relax.*

I sleep the best I have ever slept. Most people think alcohol helps a person unwind, manage stress, and sleep. I was one of them! I can tell you first hand, that the opposite is true if you give this change a chance. I used to need 9 or even sometimes 10 hours of sleep. I guess my body needed to heal overnight from the toxin. Now, I wake completely rested and refreshed. Seriously, think about that. Going alcohol-free gave me 2 hours a day of life back. That's 14 hours a week!

That's 60 hours a month which is equivalent to 2.5 days!! What?! Not only has these changes most likely extended my life by years, they will be healthy years and years that would have been slept away recovering in bed. UGH!!! I don't know about you, but this is downright unbelievable to me.

When I first started writing this book early 2020, I never would have dreamed this section would be in here. You just never know the direction of your life. Be open! The best is yet to come!

If you do take this leap, reach out and share. I would love to hear your journey. You may explore Dr. Brooke's programs on her website at: www.brookescheller.com. She has many options available including an affordable month-to-month rate. Think about it. Perhaps, I'll see you there!

21

One year, we stayed late in Maine. Late meaning, after Labor Day. It was glorious! It may seem like that word is too grand, but it is not, truly. It *IS* simply glorious. There is just no other way to describe it. As Summer inevitably came to its end, I left it all on the field, so to speak, or the dock in this case. Every long, beautiful day was spent doing something I loved, reading, writing, sunning, swimming. And nights were filled with wonder; sitting around the campfire, or laying on our neighboring boulder gazing into the clear night sky. It has been said that you can see the Aurora Borealis from here. I have not been that blessed yet, but I am hopeful to have my turn.

Speaking of turn, that is actually the point of this chapter, even its title if I were to give it one. It struck me like a chord. It was late August that very year when the strangest phrase was spoken. It made a big impact on my time, and life actually. The morning was gorgeous and warm, the sun was out, not a cloud in sight, we took a swim in the lake from the dock.

After dinner and before sunset, I headed out to our patio where neighbors gathered. I pulled out and pulled on a sweatshirt. A light weight one, but none the less, a long-sleeved sweatshirt.

"Brrrr", I said rubbing my arms as I joined our small crowd. "It's the turn," my neighbor said. "What?" I asked curiously. She went on to explain that *the turn* is when summer ends and fall begins.

I found out there is nothing gradual about the turn. One day is summer, the next is fall. Just like that. JUST LIKE THAT!

All the locals chimed in in agreement. Nodding their head sharing their conclusion that indeed the turn has happened. I realized then that their proclamation was weather related, but it hit me hard. Once the turn hits, there is no going back. That opportunity to jump off the floating dock (that you were scared to do) has now passed. That opportunity to night swim, passed. Drive-ins, passed. So many summer things, over. Just like that. The turn changes everything.

Tonight is different. We still light a campfire and pull out the smore fixin's. It's more of a closing ceremony than a nightly ritual. It's ok. I think.

I realize that you can't really prepare in advance for the turn. Always be ready would be my take. Live each day to its fullest because things can happen on a dime. Any second, things could change. They always do. Become resilient. Live life present, live life here in the moment. Not the past for too long, not the future for too long, be present.

Sure, it's natural to wander back from time to time, but to cherish, not to regret or feel shame. Forgive others. Definitely forgive yourself. Thank your body for bringing you to this point. You survived. Everything that was meant to take you out failed. You are standing.

Don't dwell too much on the future. Plan a little, but don't be too rigid. Be flexible. Be open to grow, change, adjust plans, and especially your mind. You don't have to be *everyone's* best friend. Be your *own* best friend for sure.

Find your passion, enjoy your days and your people. Prioritize your health, mind, body and spirit. Feed all three of these daily, nourish them well. We have all been through a lot; individually and collectively. It's time to heal, and enjoy.

I love you, my readers. I see you. We are in this life together. You are not alone. Even if we never meet, I am here for you.

Epilogue

Dear Regret,

I have heard you speaking to my heart too many times. I silence you today. You lost access to my mind and body.

You were there on those nights. The nights I would sneak out of bed after everyone was asleep in the house. The nights I would just think and cry, and cry and think. I thought if I just cried hard enough and long enough that you, regret, would go away. Those days and nights are over.

*I have processed my past while **in** the present, without spiraling into an abyss of sadness. A therapist told me once that 'your children will only be as well as you are.' I believe that.*

I am healed, whole and forgiven. I release myself of guilt, shame and any burden I carry. I do this for them, my family, and I do this for me.

The trauma leading up to this moment in my life is no longer swept under the rug. I know it as fact. I also know it as just a piece of my past, not as the entirety. There was a girl who existed before the trauma, THAT GIRL.

She is back.

Sincerely,

Me xo

Stephanie Connors

Books available at:

www.amazon.com/author/stephanieconnors

Contact at:

stephanieannconnors@gmail.com

Facebook:

https://www.facebook.com/connorswrites

Instagram:

@stephanieconnors

Twitter:

@Stephwrites

Clubhouse:

@stephaniec2022

Made in the USA
Columbia, SC
21 December 2022